THE POWER OF GOALS

The secret to getting **everything you want**
(faster than you ever thought possible)

Daniel J. Martin

Copyright © 2021 Daniel J. Martin

All rights reserved. No part of this publication may be reproduced, distributed, or transmitted in any form or by any means, including photocopying, recording, or other electronic or mechanical methods, nor via the public distribution of the original or copies of the work by sale, lease, or rental, without the prior written permission of the copy-right holder.

ISBN 979-8713282578

A goal without a plan is just a wish.

— Antoine de Saint-Exupéry

CONTENTS

Introduction: The formula for success 1

Chapter 1: Why we need goals 11

    The most common problems when setting goals 14

    The pillars of a great goal 22

Chapter 2: Setting the right goals 29

    Decide what you want 30

    Start with a big, realistic dream 31

    Wrong reasons for wanting what you want 38

    Right reasons for wanting what you want 40

Chapter 3: Get a map 45

    Benefits of planning your goals 47

    Features of a good action plan 50

    The essence of the planning process 60

    Divide your goals into long-, mid-, and short-term goals 62

Chapter 4: Insure your goals! 67

    Take 100% of the responsibility 68

    Beliefs and visualization 73

    Align your goals with your values 75

    Apply zero-based thinking 76

    Measure your progress 78

Associate with the right people 79

Manage your time effectively 82

The truth about motivation 84

Chapter 5: If you fall down seven times, get up eight! ... 89

Look at failure from a different point of view 93

Learn to deal with criticism 98

Conclusions 105

Your opinion matters 109

DOWNLOAD THE AUDIOBOOK FREE!

If you would rather enjoy The Power of the Goal on the go, you can download its audio version with your Audible Free 30-Day Trial!

TO DOWNLOAD GO TO:

https://geni.us/pog-audiobook

Introduction

The formula for success

Ever since I was a child, I have been known for achieving everything I set out to do. I was lucky enough to be born with that gift.

I don't mean to say that I was good at everything I did, or that I had some extraordinary built-in talent. My gift was perseverance.

If there was something I wanted, sooner or later I found a way to get it. Unfortunately, it wasn't until the age of thirty that I started to know what I really wanted.

It's not that I wasted thirty years of my life chasing after the wrong goals: I think they were years of great learning, in which I also did great things. But I would have loved to come across a book like this much earlier. However, like so many other people, it took hitting rock bottom before I could change the course of my life.

A journey of self-discovery

At just over twenty-eight years old, I had achieved everything I had set out to do up to that point. I had graduated from college, traveled the world, earned about three times more than the rest of my friends, and had a beautiful girlfriend... Basically, everything society had led me to believe success was about. Almost everyone I knew would have traded their lives for mine in an instant.

I'm not going to deny it: I was happy. I always have been.

Then, due to a series of unexpected and temporary circumstances, I «luckily» fell into a mild depression: the first and only one I've had so far. I felt so terrible that I decided to make an appointment with a psychologist, because I had begun having anxiety attacks and was fearing for my health.

However, a week before my first consultation I received an unexpected email from an old friend of mine from my backpacking days. We used to talk occasionally, but that particular email came at the right time. He told me that he had moved to Las Vegas (he's from Israel) and he asked how I was doing.

Ordinarily, I would have told him I was fine – but for some reason, I decided to tell him that I wasn't well. I told him I was going through a rough time, and that I had an appointment with a psychologist the following week.

In his next email, he simply asked for my phone number, and a few minutes later, he called me. We talked for half an hour, reminiscing on old times and not touching too much on the subject of my depression.

Ten minutes after I hung up, I got a text from my friend (this was before the days of WhatsApp), and our conversation went like this:

- Daniel, do you know what would help you a lot right now? Traveling to the United States. It's a wonderful country. Trust me, you'd love it!
- WOW! I'm sure I would! It's something I've wanted to do since I was a little boy, and I don't doubt that someday I will.
- No – I mean, come visit me. My house is your house. You won't want for anything here, and I'm sure I can help you get out of the situation you're in.

- Thank you so much, Gili! You know what? I'm going to start saving, and as soon as I can, I'll come see you.
- You don't have to save anything. I've got you covered.
- OK... Well, give me a couple of months to get organized and I'll let you know.

(10 minutes went by with no answer)

- I just sent you an email with the tickets. You leave the day after tomorrow.

Throughout my life, I have had many adventures, as I continually strive to get out of my comfort zone. But this one was, without a doubt, one of the most impactful for me.

As I rushed to get my passport in record time, with a picture in which I look like an *Al Qaeda* terrorist (you know the face of someone who's just spent several weeks confined to their home with depression?), convinced my family that nothing strange was going on and that I wasn't about to be kidnapped —without being too convinced of it myself— and gathered some cash to spend two weeks in a foreign country, I could never have imagined what that trip would entail.

Honestly, I thought it was going to be a simple vacation to clear my mind, a change of scenery to come back home with renewed energy: and it was indeed all those things, but it ended up being so much more besides. There was something else there; something special that changed the course of my life.

My friend, who at the time was around fifty years old, while I was not yet thirty, was a self-made multimillionaire, and like many other people who have achieved success on their own merits, one of his greatest sources of satisfaction consisted of helping other people in whom he saw potential to follow in his steps, saving them years of effort and failure.

It was a fun two weeks, full of all kinds of activities that my friend had planned for me, in which we also made the most of every «break» by having interesting conversations, at times very meaningful and deep. We cruised around, driving from one side of the city to the other, always with a perfectly curated playlist on the stereo, and I stayed up late every night in the living room by myself reading some of the books that my friend had left lying around that he thought might interest me.

If I had to summarize what I learned on that trip, I would do so by applying what I call the **formula for success**:

1. Work out exactly what you want.
2. Find out the price you have to pay to get it.
3. Draw up a written plan for achieving it.

Why this book?

I am aware not everyone is going to be «lucky» enough to hit rock bottom in time or at the right time, or to have a rich, altruistic friend who's there for them and ready when this happens to show them the way forward.

So, this book will be your «rich friend».

Ever since that trip, I have applied this formula to tremendous effect. I've watched my life change for the better. I earned more and learned more daily. I went from being a depressed individual to being a highly confident and able individual. I learned to know what I wanted and how to get it. That's exactly why I have written this book for you: to teach you how to achieve more than you ever thought you could.

In this guide, not only will I tell you everything I learned during those two weeks of self-discovery, but everything I have continued to learn over the following ten years of my life. This knowledge has allowed me to dedicate myself professionally to helping others **set and achieve their goals** in areas such as **health, business** and **relationships;** *because if you don't maintain a balance in the three main areas of your life (health, money and love), success will be just a passing illusion.*

I hope you enjoy reading,
Daniel J. Martin

Chapter 1

Why we need goals

The trouble with not having a goal is that you can spend your life running up and down the field and never score.

— Bill Copeland

You've probably read *Treasure Island*, *Gulliver's Travels* or other books about adventures. What do you make of them? Are they just interesting, creative, imaginative stories? Yes, most of them are fictional, yet almost all of them teach a lesson —if you want to find treasure, you need the right map. The character with the right map and the right tools almost always succeeds.

So, why don't we apply the same principles in real life? Why do we attempt to succeed without a map, without a plan for success?

Many people spend decades of their lives doing the same thing over and over, never stopping to consider where their lives are headed, or where they really want to be. They get up in the morning, go to the same job (one that's slowly killing them), and perform the same tasks, which don't bring them any satisfaction, over and over again before going back to bed to repeat the same routine the next day.

Conversely, other people are aware that there are better places to be in. They know they want to enjoy certain luxuries and comforts. They want to enjoy greater wellbeing, to have a nice life and enough money to travel the world and see different places. The problem is they don't have a plan, only vague dreams that they think they'd like to pursue, but for which they don't set any concrete goals.

Most people can be categorized in one of these two groups: people who don't know where they want to go, or people who do, but don't know how to get there. Too often, they end up spending half of their lives finding the right goals for them, before spending the other half looking for the right map for those goals. Even if they manage to achieve them, it's usually too late for them to fully enjoy the fruits of their labor.

You can't afford to belong to either one of these groups any longer; their memberships guarantee you a life of stress and frustration. Life does not have to be that hard. If you want to achieve success and enjoy a happy existence, it is imperative that you learn to set goals and draw up the right plans to achieve them.

Many people make mistakes in setting their goals and never recover from them. It's easier to pick yourself up from setbacks in the course of executing plans than it is from the mistakes you make when you've set the wrong goals. Such mistakes may have to do with the timing of the goals, the nature of them, or the way you achieve them.

In this book, I'll teach you everything you need to know both to set and to achieve your goals – so, first of all, I need to show you the mistakes you may have made or be making still!

The most common problems when setting goals

«I never figured I'd need help with setting my goals». Most people think like this, but not realizing there are better ways to do things does not absolve us of the responsibility to learn. It is true that the human brain is wired to think in terms of self-sufficiency, but it's better to be aware of the potential pitfalls beforehand.

So, what are the most common mistakes we make?

1. Right goal, wrong reasons.

Yes, you read that right. You can want the right thing for the wrong reasons. Many people fail because the reasons for their goals are wrong. When you pursue something for the wrong reasons, two things are bound to happen: either you don't achieve the thing at all, or you do, but fail to derive the fulfillment you thought you would get from the achievement of said goal. You'd have what you've always wanted, but still wouldn't feel satisfied. What follows in either case is unhappiness and frustration.

It means that all your time and effort go to waste, and that's not a good way to lead your life. That is why, later in this book, I will teach you how to set your goals for the right reasons.

2. Underestimating the price to be paid.

Underestimating what you need to do in order to get to your goals is one of the most common problems people face. It is also often a costly mistake, too, and one that can drain you of all your energy. It often happens because your plan is ill-suited for the goals you have set for yourself, because if you are convinced that your goals are right, you will continue to try and fail until you lose all motivation and willpower.

Insufficient initial research can hide the true magnitude of the task required to achieve your purpose, and each step then becomes an unexpected challenge for which you were not prepared. It takes you by surprise, throws you off balance, and before you can recover, you'll have run out of steam. That is often the first ingredient in the recipe for failure. For all this, you need to know in advance the exact price you'll have to pay to attain your goals, and be ready to pay that price.

3. Lack of commitment.

This contrasts with the above problems, where individuals are willing to give their all for the cause – the right one, yes, but in the wrong way, or for the wrong reasons. In this case, however, they may not be willing to sacrifice anything at all. Have you ever heard it said that «commitment is what transforms a promise into reality» or that «there's no abiding success without commitment»? Well, these are facts. When it comes to goals and objectives, if you don't commit to reaching them, and you're not consistent with your own commitment, you'll see them slip through your fingers.

Commitment to your goals is a prerequisite for achieving them. It is only logical that when something requires a good deal of commitment, and you give very little, you will inevitably fail. If your commitment is lacking, you will only make shoddy attempts to approach your destination – that is, you will fail to give your best if you're unwilling to make the necessary sacrifices.

4. Fear of failure.

If you are afraid of the water, you will never leave the shore. Are you more worried about failing than you are interested in success? Are you scared that you will fail horribly? Fear is a paralyzing emotion that prevents you from acting – sometimes completely – and makes your goals appear scary instead of inviting.

Fear of failure is truly a pandemic. We have all been brought up to treasure success and dread failure, but we forget that failure itself is a part of success. Failure shouldn't be the death of your dreams, but a wake-up call for you to try harder or do better. Failing doesn't mean you'll never make it, just that the current plan isn't working and you need to revise it. You need to understand the role of failure in success; once you do that, it will cease to be an obstacle.

5. Negativity.

Negative thoughts greatly affect your mental and emotional state. Negativity saps the positive emotions and energy that fuel your efforts to live a better life. It also makes it impossible to maintain your focus and concentration for long, as it provides you with a long list of excuses for not doing the things you know you should do. What's worse, negativity is contagious. Moving in the wrong circles can make it very difficult to generate the necessary motivation to achieve your goals. Negativity is the result of letting bad energies pervade your psyche. If you allow these negative energies to take over completely, you'll be at the mercy of negativity and it will be tremendously difficult to pursue any dream.

6. Lack of confidence.

Self-confidence and self-esteem go hand in hand. You can't lack self-esteem and have confidence in yourself at the same time. Together, they help you determine how much faith you have in your goals, plans and ability to make things work.

Self-esteem is about how much you think you deserve your dreams. It is your own measurement of your worth. If your self-esteem levels are low, you're probably afraid that your goals are too ambitious, you'll worry that you won't measure up, and you'll think that anyone else would be more worthy of achieving those plans or dreams you have for yourself. If you don't believe in yourself enough, you won't be able to sustain your efforts to achieve success.

Self-esteem and competence are the fundamental pillars of confidence. It gives you belief in your dreams, plans and uniqueness; competence makes you believe in your abilities. When you lack confidence, you move haltingly, unable to make decisions quickly and efficiently. You spend too much time second-guessing decisions you've already made, and when it's time to take risks, you will most likely choose the safest option. If your goals are affected by your lack of confidence, you will live your life waiting for the validation of others and that, in the end, will ultimately impact how much you can do.

7. Ignorance.

The best goals and plans are laid out from a position of knowledge. For instance, if you want to set goals for your business, you need to know all the information about your industry. You cannot set plans and goals based on intuition alone. You need to look at events from the past, current trends, your present abilities and strengths, and future projections. An inaccurate map is as useless as having no map, and inaccurate maps exist because of false information and ignorance.

Ignorance is not bliss, as the saying goes – at least, not in the context of goal-setting and achieving. It is a state of lack of knowledge or know-how, which limits you and can keep you stagnant.

The only way to defeat ignorance is by learning and acquiring information. Your goal should ignite in you a healthy obsession to learn all you can about it. For instance, if your goal is good health, then you'll need to gather as much information as you can about healthy habits. It's the only way you'll be able to plan correctly.

The pillars of a great goal

Now that you know the mistakes you should avoid, you need to know the pillars of a great goal: the things you need to put into practice to ensure that your goals are easier to attain.

1. The right goal.

You need to choose the right goals for the right reasons. If you choose the right goals, but for the wrong reasons, you will find no joy in achieving them. If you choose the wrong goals, even if you do it for the right reasons, you will end up frustrated and exhausted, chasing after mirages. In both cases, failure is guaranteed.

That's why you need a suitable goal, based on your true values and aspirations.

2. A great plan.

Dreaming big is simple. Making a plan to achieve those dreams is more complicated. Your goal is a destination you want to get to; your plan is the map to that destination. You can't reach your destination if you don't know the way there.

Knowing the way involves drawing up a good plan that covers most contingencies you are likely to encounter. No plan is perfect, and there are many variables that will change as you progress, but your initial plan should be good enough to cover most of these potential setbacks.

A good plan should spell out your goals, break them down into achievable short-term milestones, and define which markers you'll use to measure your progress. In other words, a good plan complements a good goal. With a good plan, you will be able to visualize your goal, see it divided into easily achievable steps, and measure your progress toward its achievement.

3. The right knowledge.

Without the knowledge needed to set and implement goals, you've got no chance of success. Being equipped with enough information can mean the difference between having to close your business and being the benchmark in your sector, for example. However, you can't expect to obtain the right knowledge if you don't go out and get it. Many people have similar goals. The only way to stand out in a hyper-competitive world is to acquire and accumulate more knowledge than most people, and then use it in the right way. Adequate knowledge ensures that you have the necessary tools to attain your goals.

4. Motivation and perseverance.

Nothing good ever comes easy. Achieving your goals is undoubtedly a very good thing; therefore, you can expect it to come with some challenges. Yes, even with a good plan, achieving your goals will bring with it challenges for which you need to be prepared. Remember that your plan is just an answer to some of the many variables in the complex equation of life, and the challenges will come mostly from variables beyond your control.

When these challenges rear their ugly heads – and they will – whether you give up or keep fighting will depend on your level of motivation, rooted in your reasons for wanting to achieve your goals.

If your motivation is strong enough, you will be able to look beyond your present challenges and fight for a better future.

Motivation, therefore, plays a decisive role in your ability to persevere. Due to our constant search for instant gratification, when something is not going according to plan, we find it very easy to give up and focus on something else. This can be a big problem, because you need to focus on your goals if you want to succeed. Motivation will be the fuel that ensures you remain interested, enthusiastic and focused on achieving your goals.

Chapter summary

Setting goals and achieving them is a process fraught with pitfalls and setbacks. The bigger the goal is, the greater the challenges – but the sweeter the victory. You need the right map, and a burning motivation to fuel your way towards your goals. Life itself is a journey towards your goals, your destination. Failing to prepare yourself adequately for that journey is going to either sidetrack you or see you quitting at the first hurdle.

Why you need goals

- You need to set the right goals in order to maximize your potential and your interest in completing them.
- Make sure your goals are aligned with your true values and aspirations. If not, you won't find any satisfaction in attaining them.

- Educate and inform yourself. You need to know what you're up against and the price you'll need to pay.
- Commit to paying that price.
- Look for the right motivation within you; this will prevent you from throwing in the towel halfway through.

Chapter 2

Setting the right goals

All successful men and women are big dreamers. They imagine what their future could be, ideal in every respect, and then they work every day toward their distant vision, that goal or purpose.

— Brian Tracy

Now that you know the most common problems people face when it comes to setting and achieving goals, it's time to learn how to set the right goals.

Decide what you want

How do you know what you want in life? There are so many things to want—love, money, career success, financial success, fame etc. Are these the right things to want in life? There's nothing wrong with wanting any of these things – or all of them. In fact, they are more or less the «ultimate» goals. We all want to love and be loved. We want to get to the top of our career and, possibly, set new standards for those behind us on the path to success. We want to be financially successful, to have the certainty that we can retire early in life. All of these are perfectly normal things to want.

The issue is actually that if you have many goals in each of these areas, you subconsciously start working towards all of them all at once. When you work like this, you end up losing the potential to have an impact. Instead of making vague statements about your goals, or chasing several at once, decide what you want right now and go for that. Focusing your skills and qualities on specific goals is better than making scattered attempts at many things at a time.

Start with a big, realistic dream

Yes – start with a dream. Now, this doesn't mean you should make your goals a fantasy. Every goal should start with a dream, but it shouldn't end there. Castles in the air, however beautiful they may be, will never be more than mere illusions unless you build solid foundations for them to stand upon. All ideas, before they can stand on their own, have to be conceived, and the stage of conception is important because it dictates how much motivation you can generate. If you create a vivid, absorbing and realistic dream, you will have more enthusiasm to get out there and make it happen.

You can picture yourself as the president of a large multinational company, the best quarterback in the world, a Nobel Prize or Oscar winner, or, equally possible if you don't believe in yourself, as an utter failure. How much you believe in your dreams will determine, to a great extent, how many of those dreams you'll be able to achieve. Believing in your dreams gives you a reason to work hard and try to make them come true. You may still not make it for reasons completely out of your control, but you will certainly have a greater chance at doing so. This is the foundation of every successful goal: a vision of the goal.

Now, let's talk about various aspects of life where you can set goals, and what possible goals you could set for each of them. I have not arranged these aspects in order of importance, because every one of them is as important as the next. For instance, your career impacts your finances, and both will suffer the consequences of poor health, since all of these areas are interconnected.

1. Career.

Where do you see yourself in five years? Visualize yourself in the near future. Five years is a long enough time to be considered a long-term goal, but close enough not to lose its motivational power—it's not that far off. If you know where you want to be in five years' time, for example, then you know where you need to be in three years' time and what you have to do to get there. If you know your dream for the next three years, then you know what you need to do this year, this month, this week and even today. This means you can start doing the necessary things right away.

So, I ask you again: professionally speaking, where do you see yourself in the next five years?

Do you want to finish law school and become a partner at a top law firm? Do you want to start and complete a doctorate? Do you want to scale your business up and delve into new endeavors? Do you want to compete in the Olympics?

Career goals are very important because they help you in at least two ways: first, they add to your net worth and increase your income and benefits; and second, they give you a sound footing to go even further and reach other goals.

Set concrete career goals that can change the way you handle your daily tasks. Instead of living in a rut, look to the future and live each day according to the dream in your mind. As the saying goes, «dress for the job you want...»

2. Finances.

What's the point in having a career or college degree if it can't directly increase your income? Goals that are directly or indirectly capable of increasing your sources or level of income should be part of your core goals. While having a master's, for example, doesn't mean that banks are going to give you money just because you flashed your university degree, it does have the potential to set you apart from the competition and land you better, more rewarding roles.

Finances are very important. As a friend once said to me, «nothing is free, not even in Freetown». The minimum level of comfort you can enjoy is directly related to your ability to pay the bills, and this, in turn, depends on how much you earn within a given period of time. The amount you earn depends on your sources and types of income. I have always taught people they should never rely on a single source of income, but rather have alternative sources of passive income that bring in cash for them.

So, when it comes to finances, your goal should be twofold: to increase your current **level of income** and to increase your **sources of income**.

These two goals will give rise to other, smaller goals you can work upon in order to increase your financial security. More and greater income means being able to not only cover your basic needs, but to also satisfy your desires – reasonably, of course – and create funds for a rainy day and for your retirement (among other things).

3. Health.

Health is wealth! Every other thing you may want in life pales in comparison to good health. This is why, at every stage in your life, you should devote proper attention to your health, get regular checkups, and develop healthy habits.

It is also important to aspire to be in good physical condition. It's not just a matter of looking good; being physically fit will keep your body healthier. Although the number of people that are choosing to take care of themselves on the outside is increasing, many are neglecting themselves on the inside; an unforgivable mistake, because the pillars of good health are not only physical, but mental and emotional, too.

Ideally, there should be a balance between body and mind, so you should set yourself goals that allow you to optimize your mental and physical health.

4. Relationships.

No man is an island. We exist as part of society, and that means we must relate and interact with others in all kinds of situations and conditions. The good thing is you have power over what sort of relationships you choose to have, because the kind of people you associate with in your private, public and professional lives will directly or indirectly influence who you are as a person. You might have heard the saying «we are the average of the five people we spend the most time with». This is why you need to set relationship goals. Draw up principles and rules for the way you relate with people; setting healthy boundaries as to what you're willing to give and receive in your relationships is also important. It will help you optimize your social life for best results.

Wrong reasons for wanting what you want

1. Unhealthy competition.

Competition is good, but not in all circumstances. Unhealthy comparisons with other people may damage your self-confidence beyond repair, and even make it impossible for you to be genuinely motivated. What you need to know is that circumstances are often unique and different even in people with similar goals, so you're not doing yourself any favors by drawing comparisons to other people – quite the opposite. Don't crave a goal just because other people have a similar target. Don't chase a goal for the sake of achieving it before other people do, because you won't find the usual feeling of success or satisfaction that should follow an achievement.

2. Seeking external approval.

Why have you set out to achieve your goals? Is it to seek the approval of other people? If the answer is yes, then you are pursuing your goals for the wrong reason. Seeking the approval of others means you lack self-esteem. It means you are living your life based on the validation of others. What happens then if you complete your goals, and the external validation you crave never comes? I'll tell you: that «success» will leave a bad taste in your mouth.

3. Envy.

Envy is a negative and toxic emotion: a type of mental bondage which blinds you to the right things in life. Wanting to achieve your goal because you envy other people that have done the same is harmful to your mental health and self-esteem. It arises from the same feeling of inadequacy that drives a person to toxic behavior.

Mind you, there is nothing wrong with wanting to achieve as much as Bill Gates, or Elon Musk, or Colonel Sanders. What *is* wrong is wanting it simply because you think you're better than those who have done it. That's envy: feeling that you are more deserving of the success that others have achieved.

Envious people face a terrible problem: if they fail, envy will take hold of them to the point of making them sick. If they succeed, they will immediately find something else to envy.

Right reasons for wanting what you want

All of your goals should be personalized and tailored to your needs and circumstances. Life is divided into stages, and the same applies to your goals. You need a college degree before you get a master's degree, so while your long-term vision may include postgraduate studies, completing an undergraduate degree should be your immediate goal.

Your goals should help you become a better, happier and more successful individual, and this can only be achieved by being authentic and having authentic goals and aspirations. The responsibility for your life and goals lies with you, so your goals should be tailored for maximum self-improvement and success.

For instance, your career goals should be about climbing the corporate or professional ladder you want, not fulfilling the expectations others have for you. If they intersect, that's fine. If they don't, go for your own goals. In the same vein, you deserve to love and be loved, so your relationship goals should be about yourself just as much as they are about your partner. Your romantic goals should not allow a toxic relationship to move forward. These are just a few examples, but I'm sure you get the idea. Your goals should be yours and for you. Only if they are tailored to you will they allow you to enjoy the life you've always dreamed of.

In addition, we have a moral duty to help other people around us, so your goals should also leave room to help others. Help can be given in many ways and, of course, it doesn't necessarily have to be financial. You could help others by becoming their mentor, guiding them and lending them a hand. If you start a business as an entrepreneur and end up amassing a small fortune, you could make it a goal to help fifty or a hundred people achieve similar success in their businesses over the next few years.

Most importantly, your goals should give you enormous personal satisfaction when completed; attaining them should bring you fulfillment and joy. This should be the ultimate purpose of every goal you pursue.

Chapter summary

Many people chase too many goals at the same time, making it hard for them to focus on one at a time. You may also have the right goals for the wrong reasons. It's important that you make sure you are pursuing those goals for the right reasons, and that you set specific goals for each of the major areas of your life: work, finances, health and relationships.

Setting the Right Goals

- What are your goals? What things have you been pursuing for the last few years? Are they suitable goals?
- Decide what you want. There is no time for vagueness and ambiguity. You need to know what you want in life now.
- Start with a big, realistic dream. Ensure that your goals really interest you, motivate you and are important to you.

- Why do you want those goals? Make sure your motivation comes from the desire to make a positive impact on your life and other people's lives. Unhealthy competition, seeking external validation, and envy, will render your goals meaningless and empty.

Chapter 3

Get a map

Our goals can only be reached through a vehicle of a plan in which we must fervently believe and upon which we must vigorously act.

— Pablo Picasso

You cannot get to your goal without the right plan. The first thing to realize is that, while you need big and bold long-term goals, you must be willing to break them into smaller, attainable mini-goals, and then plan around these smaller milestones.

If you pursue your goals without a definite plan detailing your approach, you won't be able to overcome quickly enough any unforeseen events that may arise. It's easy to say that you want to get in shape and achieve a slim figure, but if you don't have a plan that specifies what kind of food you should eat and the exercise routine you should follow, you'll never reach that goal. It's not enough to say you want to get rich; you need a plan that will guide you along the road to getting rich. Every goal has some basic requirements, and you must put these in place.

So, what should a good plan look like?

In the previous chapter, you learned how to create a goal and also that you should set goals for different areas of your life: career, finances, health and relationships. There's nothing wrong with having goals in each of these areas, but to plan effectively, each of these goals should be made up of the sum of several smaller goals that you can achieve progressively.

Benefits of planning your goals

1. It helps you refine your ideas.

If, at this very moment, you were to pick up a pen and paper to write down your goals, you would realize that many more ideas will suddenly come to you. In addition, getting into the habit of writing down your goals will prevent you, among other things, from forgetting important ideas. Planning your goals in writing makes it easier for you to review and redefine them as much as necessary before taking any type of action.

2. It gives you an overall view of your goal.

With your goals laid out, and the steps to achieving each one detailed, you'll get a full picture of where you are and where you need to be. If you have more than one goal, planning your goals also allows you to visualize the connections between them. It enables you to properly assess your goals and determine which one should come first based on what needs to be done.

3. It helps you identify pitfalls in your plans.

Once you have a perfectly defined plan laid out in front of you, not only will it be easier for you to determine what needs to be done, but also what *not* to do. Planning will help you anticipate potential obstacles as you try to determine which actions are most conducive to achieving each of your goals. An action plan for your goal, simply put, helps you identify flaws in your plans and obstacles to making them happen.

4. It helps you measure your progress.

A good action plan contains a detailed description of what you need to do, when, how, and what results to expect. With those details in place, you have a yardstick for measuring your progress towards achieving your main goal. Think of it like taking different courses at a university, where there are a certain number of exams you need to take or papers to submit each year. Your performance in your first year determines your average grade for the course. Add in what you do in your second year, and you'll have a new grade point average. As you move through the program, you'll have an awareness of how well you've done, and how much remains to be done.

5. It saves you time and resources.

Based on everything we've seen so far, one thing is clear: a good plan can save you a lot of time and effort. When you plan your moves in advance, you'll avoid obvious mistakes. We can't deny the fact that it's easier to get into something than it is to get out of it. By carefully planning for your goals, you'll take the necessary precautions before committing your resources to a project that may or may not come to fruition.

Features of a good action plan

What features does a plan need to have for it to be considered excellent?

1. Start by clearly writing out your goal.

A solid action plan begins with the desired goal clearly written out. Yes, **you need to put your plan in writing**, because this gives you a clear vision of where you're headed. You need to know your eventual goal before you can break it down into smaller milestones.

You'd be surprised by the number of people that have only short-term goals, but none long-term. They simply move from wanting one thing to wanting the next. They may want a new car for some months until they either get it or give up, and then switch their attention to losing those extra pounds, for example. These smaller goals may be wonderful, but without a clear, big, long-term goal, those people might look back and find it hard to link all these small, isolated successes to a life of purpose – which can end up making them feel empty. So, you need to write down your ultimate goal in a statement that summarizes every smaller goal or milestone you'll need to complete in order to achieve your main goal or objective.

A properly written goal should not express a fantasy or a dream—it should express a concrete goal; a big one, yes, but realistic. This is done by providing as much detail as possible, and avoiding any vagueness or ambiguity. For example, this «declaration of intent» should not just state that you want to achieve financial independence or increase your income. Instead, it should provide clear and specific measures. It should state the exact amount by which you need or want to increase your income, and the specific timeframe within which you want to achieve said increase. This is crucial for measurability and quantification.

«Boosting my monthly profits from $1,500 to $3,000 from two different sources of income in the next two years» is a better goal than «I want to earn more money» – which is more of a wish than a goal. Writing down your goal will also regularly remind you of your target, keeping you focused and motivated by it. You can even leave this goal written in a visible place as a reminder: on the refrigerator door, on the bathroom mirror, as the wallpaper on your computer or cell phone, and so on. Having your goal in writing and in sight will keep it alive.

2. Make a list of what needs to be done.

Take increase in income as an example. There are several things to be done, such as cutting unnecessary expenses, investing more in marketing, developing new skills or creating a new brand entirely. Your plan should contain all of these aspects, each of them a milestone that must be completed. It is the achievement of each of these tasks that will lead to your overall goal of increasing your income. So, a good plan should list and detail each of the tasks or activities to be performed in order to achieve your goal.

3. Make a list of who needs to do what.

The fact that you have a personal goal does not mean certain smaller goals within that cannot be performed by others for you. As a sales manager, for example, increasing your income may depend on the amount you earn as a bonus for the number of sales. If you have to reach a certain threshold to qualify for this bonus, then you certainly have to up your managerial game, because what that needs to be done doesn't depend on you alone—you have sales reps who need to make sales, and a team to manage your data and track sales figures. It's rare to be able to complete a major goal by yourself, since normally, various people need to be involved in one way or another – you need to understand the roles to be fulfilled, and who's going to fulfil them.

4. Decide how it needs to be done.

It's not enough to know what to do and who's going to do it. You also need to specify how it's going to be done. In fact, this point highlights the main reason why you need an action plan for achieving your goal: because it details the steps to follow to achieve it. For each smaller goal you have identified, you need to specify how it has to be done. For example, if you want to start blogging, how do you plan to make money from it? What's your strategy? What niche should you venture into? Do you plan to use Google AdSense or direct digital marketing? Will you be selling products on your blog? Do you have a plan for lead generation and email marketing? Which hosting service will you use? Your plan should answer all of these questions, and many more.

5. Outline when it should be done.

Yes, after determining what is to be done, who's going to do it and how it has to be done, the next question is *when* it should be done. There should be a sequence and logical order for everything you need to do; you can't just run haphazardly after your goals. You need to have a clear schedule for when each goal should be attained, because if you don't, you may end up putting the cart before the horse, as it were. Your timeframe should include both a schedule indicating when the execution of each minor goal should begin, and your estimated time for completion.

6. State your expectations.

What are the expectations for each of the smaller goals you have identified above? You need to state the expected result, with concrete details, as well as the minimum requirements that must be met before you can consider a goal completed.

For example, in order to increase your income through a blog, you first need to learn the basics of blogging, and then proceed to create and manage your own. You can set a timeframe for this, and some minimum requirements that must be met, such as «being able to have the first draft of my blog ready by the end of the third week of learning». This way, if you have not achieved the desired results by then, you will know how far behind you are, and how much faster you need to go.

7. Highlight the weaknesses and potential threats to your plan.

Do your plans have weaknesses? Of course, every plan can be improved upon, so it's very likely there are certain weaknesses in your plan. There is no such thing as a perfect plan; you must know this. There are many variables in achieving a goal, and not all of them will be under your direct control. Let me give you a very straightforward example: if you create a blog and have to fill it with content, you can choose to write it yourself or outsource it. The second option means you may have to rely on a freelance ghostwriter to deliver as scheduled. This could lead to delays outside your control, and in turn threaten your blog's performance. Therefore, it's a potential weakness or threat that you should take into account and, if possible, mitigate.

Every plan has at least one weak point. You can't really expect to fix or eliminate them all, but you can try to anticipate them and make adjustments to time, effort, strategy or cost to reduce their impact. Even if you don't have a clear solution for your weaknesses, being aware of their potential presence, and planning accordingly, is already moving in the right direction.

8. Include details for each item on the list.

I have already mentioned that, when drawing up your plan, you need to identify the smaller goals or milestones that you'll need to achieve cumulatively before you reach your main goal. This is why some authors have described every great plan as a 'multi-tasking' plan, meaning that you'll have meticulous plans within a larger, detailed plan.

While your plan for the main goal will indicate the specific milestones or goals to be achieved first, you can provide more details for each of the specific goals separately. This higher level of detailing requires paying the utmost attention to a large number of aspects, and the first and foremost of these is knowledge. Acquiring the necessary knowledge is essential: you can't start a blogging business unless you know about online marketing; you can't begin your home rental agency if you're not familiar with real estate, and so on.

9. The plan is for you, not the other way round.

It is said that the law is made for man, and not man for the law. This also applies here: the plan is made for you, not you for the plan.

Understanding this will prevent you from blindly following a plan. If something goes wrong or there's a change in the variables, you should be bold enough to make adjustments, provide alternatives or draw up a new plan entirely. Your interests should be the main priority. Don't let emotions keep you clinging to a plan until it's too late.

The essence of the planning process

Okay – let me offer you a reality check. You can't achieve success by following the plan you've drawn up to the letter. Why? Because factors are never permanent, and you will have to continuously adapt to new realities. Plans are based on our assumptions of what the variables are at the time of making them.

Think of plans as going to war against an enemy. You gather as much intelligence as possible about the enemy—the size of their army, the type of weapons and ammunition they'll use, their past successes and their allies. You prepare your battle plan based on that knowledge, and then you go to war. On the battlefield, you discover that not all your information about the enemy was correct. You might have planned to face a large army but ended up facing a smaller one, or vice versa; perhaps their weaponry turned out to be greater than you thought; they had unexpected allies, and so on. At this point, you're going to have to modify your original plan if you want to stop the enemy outmaneuvering you and defeating you in battle. Life plans work in the same way.

The moment you start implementing your plan, you may realize that you had underestimated or overestimated certain things. This will require you to modify not only your approach to the goal, but also the resources necessary to achieve it. In fact, in some cases, you may end up having to modify 50% of your plan, if not more.

So, what is the point of having a plan in the first place? The answer lies in the planning process.

The plan is not as important as the planning process itself. The latter requires that you do careful, meticulous research, understand the workings of certain variables, consider possible alternatives to your chosen approach, and critically appraise your goals and their viability. The planning process equips you with the willingness and skills necessary to adapt to the changing circumstances of the environment, which will maximize your chances of attaining your goals.

Divide your goals into long-, mid-, and short-term goals

The most effective way to achieve your goals is by splitting your big goals into smaller ones. Any good plan must include long-term, mid-term and short-term goals. Splitting your big, or long-term, goals into smaller weekly or daily ones will make it much easier for you to focus on them and consequently to achieve them.

Start with the long-term goals. What do you want to achieve in the next five years? These big goals take time to attain: buying a home, finishing college, or starting your own business. Your long-term goals are the basis for setting your other, smaller goals, as they define where you want to be in the future. It's okay to dream big, as long as you're being realistic.

Then, continue with your mid-term goals. These will be the great steps that bring you closer to your main aims. For example, if your main aim is to buy a house, a good mid-term goal could be to save up the 15% for the deposit that the bank will require to grant you the mortgage. These goals should also have specific deadlines, as this will help you stay focused and not drift off track.

Finally, focus on the short-term goals. These are goals you can achieve with relative ease. They are actionable tasks you can start working on immediately. Set short-term goals for each quarter, for example. You can start enquiring into house prices in your area, set out to reduce your expenses, think about ways to generate more income, and so on. These simple tasks or aims will guide you towards your ultimate goal.

This chapter has dealt extensively with planning, because it is one critical aspect that many people overlook. But your goal is only as good as the effort you put into planning for it. If you don't plan at all, you will be overwhelmed by surprises and unexpected setbacks. When you draw up your plan, you're familiarizing yourself with the various routes to your goal while preparing yourself to deal with unforeseen factors, which are sure to come into play. Planning keeps you in control and gives you a map to work with.

If you don't plan out your success, you are planning your failure.

Chapter summary

You can't reach your goals if you don't have a plan for the journey ahead. You need to draw up a detailed plan that leaves as little to chance as possible, helps you anticipate setbacks, and provides you with alternatives. It should contain clear instructions and steps to follow. The planning process gives you an awareness of all the variables and factors that might crop up, and keeps you in control.

Get a map

- Start with a clear, written goal.
- List everything that needs to be done, who should do it, and how it should be done and when.
- Define your main (or long-term) goal and then break it down into smaller, mid-term or short-term goals.

Chapter 4

Insure your goals!

If you want to be happy, set a goal that commands your thoughts, liberates your energy and inspires your hopes.

— Andrew Carnegie

You've decided on your goals, been through the planning process, drawn up an integrated plan...Are you done now? Not yet!

Reaching goals involves taking risks. In life and in business, the best way to prepare for unexpected dangers is to have some kind of insurance or guarantee, so you should apply the same principle to your goals. Yes! You can insure your goals against any threat, just as you would insure your house against fire or damage.

How can you help your goals survive any challenge? Insuring your goals begins with taking responsibility and ends with finding a boundless supply of motivation. In this chapter, I'll help you work out how to do just that.

Take 100% of the responsibility

We're wired to find an excuse for any undesired situation we find ourselves in. Why did I fail my exam? Why are my business's sales plummeting? Why is my love life a mess? Why am I putting on weight? You've probably asked yourself something like this, and then automatically started looking for reasons that absolve you of all culpability.

«The questions were too hard and I didn't have enough time»; «My competitor's new marketing strategy is stealing all my customers»; «My partner is asking too much of me and I can't do anything about it»; «I eat so much junk food because I work all day and don't have time to cook». Do these sound like the answers you give yourself? Well, most of us do it; we find answers that enable us to stay guilt-free and cast blame on others. You might blame time, your job or the government, but one way or another you find ingenious ways to avoid taking responsibility and to pass the blame onto another person or factor.

You're never the problem, or the reason for the problem. You always find some way to hold others responsible for your misfortune, and so you keep making the same mistakes over and over. Until you can admit that the problem lies with you, you won't make any effort to change what it is you're doing.

Unfortunately, this also makes it harder for you to achieve your goals. Why? Because before you've even started pursuing them, you've already passed responsibility for them onto other people or factors outside your control.

As such, the first part of your insurance policy involves taking total responsibility for your goals, your plans, and the results you get. Yes – I'm telling you to start taking the blame for your mistakes. Sorry. It wasn't the questions that made you fail your test; it was your lack of effort. Your boss isn't the reason you got fired; you are. Maybe they had to make cuts and you weren't valuable enough to keep on payroll. Your partner isn't the reason you're getting fat; you are. No one's been holding a gun to your head to make you eat junk. Even when other people have harmed you, you're still at fault. Why? Because how you react to that depends on you. Only you can decide to take attacks personally and allow what others say or do to hurt you.

«We cannot choose our external circumstances, but we can always choose how we respond to them.» — Epictetus

Your reaction to things that happen in your life will determine what you can achieve. No one can wipe away your smile unless you let them; no one can make you feel miserable if you don't tolerate it. You won't gain weight if you take action to stop it happening. You won't! You are responsible for 100% of the results you obtain. Once you understand and accept this, your focus toward your goals, and your life in general, will change. When you stop passing the buck, you become more proactive and competent at fulfilling your aims. You have to accept responsibility and bear the guilt.

But be careful! Don't wallow in it. Focusing on it can be demotivating and even depressing, rather than giving you the drive to fix your mistakes. Once you've assumed that guilt, get straight back on track. If your plans don't work out, take responsibility and immediately start looking for a solution.

The difference between a successful person and an unsuccessful one is that the former takes responsibility and then tries to find a solution, while the latter refuses to be accountable and therefore doesn't try to fix what ain't broke. And even if they finally admit to the problem, they dwell on it rather than finding a way out of it.

When I say you must accept full responsibility, part of that means controlling your emotions – especially the negative ones. It's impossible not to feel them, and those «bad vibes» are actually a sign of mental fortitude and emotional intelligence. The important thing is not to get trapped in these negative feelings, but to control them and allow them to flow through you before letting them go. You can do this by maintaining a positive mindset – not just about yourself, but about others, too.

At the same time as taking responsibility, start planning a way out of failure.

Beliefs and visualization

You are a reflection of what's going on in your mind: by that, I mean that what you express through your words and actions is an accurate representation of what's really going through your head. Your mind doesn't care what you put in it. It works on the principle of «garbage in, garbage out», so if you feed your mind with positivity, you'll shine with energy and positive emotions. If, on the other hand, you fill it with negativity, you'll give off negative energy and emotions. Your mind takes what you give it and multiplies it. That's why you need to learn to use it in your favor through visualization.

What is your goal? Paying off your mortgage in full in the next four years? If so, try to visualize yourself in your house; picture yourself in that house as if you had already finished paying off the mortgage and it was completely yours, debt-free. If you want to run – or win – your first marathon, close your eyes and imagine yourself on the last stretch, fighting for first place, coming up ahead and crossing the finish line first. Let that feeling of success wash over you.

The power of visualization starts with the power of believing in yourself. If you believe you are truly capable of achieving something, then picturing yourself as if you had already done it won't be hard.

«You become what you think about most of the time.» — Brian Tracy

Yes – your actions reflect your thoughts, and your thoughts reflect what you believe about yourself. If you can keep visualizing your goals, you'll be able to reach them.

Visualization will serve as a kind of insurance for your goals, etching them into your subconscious. Once your goals are part of your psyche, your actions will drive you towards them without you even having to think about it.

Align your goals with your values

One reason why many people never achieve satisfaction is the dissonance between their actions and their values. True happiness occurs when your life on the outside is a reflection of your life on the inside: of what's going on inside you. That is to say that only when your goals are aligned with your deepest values can you be happy. So, lining up your values with your goals is another way of insuring them, because if you're doing what makes you happy, you'll never stop chasing your goals. To do this, you need to make sure your values are sincere. That's why, in earlier chapters, I insisted on setting goals that match up with your true aspirations.

Apply zero-based thinking

Are we doomed to repeating the same mistakes over and over? No! The trick is to see them from another point of view. If you still can't do that, let me teach you a powerful tool that will help you turn your mistakes into lessons: zero-based thinking. It's a technique that allows you to analyze and objectively assess your present and future decisions based on your own past experiences. The fundamental premise and starting point of this is to ask yourself the following question:

Knowing what I know today, would I make the same decision again?

Say you're not happy in your job. The effort-pay ratio isn't what you'd like it to be, your bosses and/or colleagues make your life difficult, you feel wasted and frustrated by the results you're getting... If you could go back and be offered the same job again, knowing what you know about it now, would you take it? If the answer is no, you know you need to make a change – maybe a radical one – to get yourself out of that situation. If, on the other hand, your answer is yes, even knowing the disadvantages, then you'll know you're advancing along the path your chose, though it might need a little adjustment.

If you met your current partner today, knowing everything you know about them now, would you start that relationship again? If you hadn't decided to make a certain investment, or get involved in a particular business, would you do it again knowing what you know today? And here's one more, a very useful one for defining your priorities: if some disaster or other meant you lost all of your possessions and you had to start from scratch, which things would you replace first? If there are some things you wouldn't miss, that's a sign they're not essential to you. You can do this with everything: work, people, and even memories and nostalgia that you might be clinging to.

The idea is to act preventatively today, planning strategically and trying to take your emotions out of the equation so you can avoid regret tomorrow. If you're already regretting a decision you made, this tool will help you dot the i's and work out which things you should stop doing, or start doing differently. Life is too short to keep tormenting yourself doing things you know aren't working.

Measure your progress

Do you think it's enough to set your goals, draw up a plan, put it into practice and then go to bed? Well, it's not – you also need to measure your progress. How long ago did you start your plan? How close are you to the end? Can you honestly say you've made any progress since you started?

The essence of setting a goal is to arrive at a destination, and each step you take should bring you closer to that destination. The only way to know if your plan is working is to measure your progress towards the aims you've set yourself. As I've mentioned before, your main goal is divided into other, smaller ones that you will have to implement gradually. Each smaller goal should have a concrete timeframe in which it needs to be completed. Measuring your progress will show you exactly where you are and what you should have been doing but weren't, as well as what you need to do to keep moving forward.

So, measuring your goals is one of the best ways of insuring them. If you do it right, you'll avoid drifting off track towards your goals and you'll be more likely to reach the finish line.

Associate with the right people

People in your life shouldn't be there just for the sake of it; each person should add value. This rule applies to every area of your life – but be careful not to limit that value solely to material gain. A person can be valuable in your life for the emotional support they give you. This category will include, for example, members of your family or your partner.

If you really want to move forward in life and reach your goals, you shouldn't limit yourself to your current contact network, and you can achieve this in two ways:

The first way is to eliminate any non-beneficial relationships – those that take up your time or ask too much of you, giving you little or nothing in return. Cut them out of your life. Another kind of relationship you need to nip in the bud is any that hurts you (whether physically, verbally, psychologically or emotionally). Not only do they provide no benefit, but they can actually be brutally harmful, sapping your energy and filling you with negativity.

The second is by expanding or developing new relationships. Your closest circle should only contain people who are valuable to you and help get you closer to your goals. You can achieve this expansion in two ways:

- Subtle expansion, which involves simply meeting people in your chosen field. Consider approaching the speaker of a seminar you just attended, just to thank them. That friendly gesture will make it easier for you to establish a more meaningful relationship in the future.

- There is also direct expansion. This is about people you really need in your life. It could be some new creative talent you need to hire, or a mentor to advise and guide you. Don't be afraid to approach these people. If they are truly essential to achieving your aim, you'll be sabotaging yourself if you don't do it. Remember the rule: everyone in your life should add value to it.

Manage your time effectively

Time is a difficult concept to define. It describes how an event relates to another in chronological terms. When we talk about doing something within a set period of time, what we are really saying is that we want to synchronize that activity with the development of another, or with other events. So, it's actually ourselves – not time itself – that we need to manage in order to complete activities or fulfil goals in the time that we want to. That said, to keep things simple, we'll use the term 'time management'.

The greatest threat to good time management is procrastination: «the thief of time». We tend to procrastinate when we have – or think we have – more than enough time to complete a task, or when we feel overwhelmed by it. The trick is to find a way to intentionally reduce the time available for completing it in a way that you can't then extend it arbitrarily to make up for the time you've lost.

On the other hand, when facing an overwhelming task, the easiest and most effective thing to do is to divide the task up into various stages, and assign each stage a portion of the total time available. For example, if you have to make a long journey from A to D, the complexity and distance of the journey might feel unsettling. It's a good idea, then, to break the journey up into three parts: from A to B, then B to C, and finally C to D.

It's much easier to complete a small task, and the feeling of accomplishment you get from doing so will motivate you to carry on with the next task, and then the next, until you've achieved your main aim.

As you can see, everything I've talked about here is really about you, not about time itself. This is why time management is directly linked to self-discipline.

The truth about motivation

Encarta defines motivation as «a feeling of enthusiasm, interest or commitment that makes a person want to do something, or something that inspires such a feeling». I've reproduced this definition here because I think it's very accurate, as it highlights the main point about motivation: the need for it to be self-sustained. Motivation is what gets you leaping out of bed in the morning, ready to achieve your aims; it gives you that push towards action and helps you stay on the road to success, even when you feel like you're not making any progress.

Motivation is the fuel for your engine, your body. Sometimes, achieving your aims can be tremendously complicated and costly, but if you want something enough, and you want it for long enough, nothing can stop you from getting it. Motivation is what enables you to «want it enough» and for long enough. It helps get you on your feet and keeps you going when things get tough.

To keep your motivation up, focus on your goal, visualize it, constantly picture yourself having achieved it, and remember at all times why you want it so much.

If your goal is your destination, and your plan is the map that shows you the way, then motivation is the fuel you need to get there.

Chapter summary

Setting goals and drawing up plans to achieve them is no guarantee of success. You need to insure your goals. To do that, you must take full responsibility for everything that happens to you, visualize yourself reaching your goals, and make sure they're in line with your true values. Only then will they give you the motivation you need to keep going and avoid throwing in the towel halfway.

Insure your goals

- Your progress towards your goals must be constantly measured and evaluated. You need indicators to help you do that. You can analyze each smaller milestone you've set yourself and see how many of them you've completed on schedule.
- Apply zero-based thinking to get out of situations in your life that you never would have

gotten into had you known what you know now, or at least, to help you make the necessary changes.
- Manage your time effectively. Time is a measure of success; eliminate distractions and avoid procrastinating. Focus on what you need to do and tackle tasks decisively in order to complete them as fast as possible.
- The people around you affect your ability to work toward your goals. Maintain healthy, beneficial relationships, and cut out negative people.
- Use visualization to etch your goals into your subconscious. That way, sticking to your plans will become second nature.

Chapter 5

If you fall down seven times, get up eight!

In order to succeed you must fail, so that you know what not to do the next time.

— Anthony J. D'Angelo

Imagine you're out horseback riding. Suddenly, the animal rears up on its hind legs and throws you to the ground. What do you do? Do you just sit there, refusing to get back on? Or do you try to work out why you fell off, and get back on?

Let's relate this metaphor to a real-life story.

In the early 2000s, J. K. Rowling became the first female author in history to become a multimillionaire, thanks to her critically-acclaimed Harry Potter series. But this success story was anything but easy. In fact, the writer had so many problems that no one would have blamed her for giving up and abandoning her goals.

Joanne Rowling was born into a working class English family on July 31st 1965. From early childhood, Joanne was always interested in stories, and would write fantasy fiction to read to her sister Dianne. But her efforts and wishes to make a living as a writer didn't garner her much support from her parents.

In 1982, she took her entrance exams for Oxford University, but she didn't get in and ended up studying French at the University of Exeter, intending to find work later as a bilingual secretary. After graduation, she got a job as a translator for Amnesty International, but she didn't enjoy secretarial work. She simply wasn't born for it – so she quit!

In 1990, the inspiration for the theme of the Harry Potter books came to Joanne while she was waiting for a train from Manchester to London. Sadly, that same year, her mother Anne died following a ten-year battle against multiple sclerosis. This greatly affected Joanne's life and her writing. To escape her grief, and after reading an ad in the The Guardian newspaper, she moved to Oporto in Portugal to teach English. Within eighteen months, she had married a Portuguese journalist, conceived her daughter Jessica, and got a divorce. In late 1993, she moved back to Britain without a penny to her name, with no clear plans for the future and dependent on government welfare.

But despite the difficulties she faced, Joanne kept her passion for writing alive, and in 1995, her first manuscript was finally finished and ready for publication. So, publishing houses must have been fighting for the rights to her book, right? Not in the slightest! In fact, twelve big publishing houses rejected her work. It was a small company who finally took a gamble on her and published her book – but not before advising her to start looking for another job, because she wasn't a very talented writer.

And the rest...is history.

It's easy to look back at similar success stories throughout history and focus only on the victories, but you must remember the failures and obstacles that those people had to overcome to get there. J. K. Rowling suffered from depression, lost her mother, went through a marriage breakdown and was left penniless while taking care of her daughter. But she never gave up – she knew that all the setbacks and adverse circumstances she faced were valuable lessons taught to her by failure.

When failure is your teacher, you pay more attention, because you'll do anything to avoid failing again. You can't succeed without failing along the way. In the words of Sir Winston Churchill, «Success consists of going from failure to failure without loss of enthusiasm». So, instead of focusing on falling off your horse, concentrate on getting straight back on.

Setbacks can happen in many different ways. But even then, none of the setbacks you'll have to face will be new. Many people will have faced – and overcome – them before you. In this chapter, we'll look at how to deal with these hitches or unexpected situations to help you achieve your goals.

Look at failure from a different point of view

97% of people have just one way of viewing failure: as a defeat. This is one of the main reasons why they stagnate and realize they've achieved little or nothing over the course of their lives. The remaining 3% see failure differently, and that's what helps them succeed over and over again in life. If we could choose, I'm sure we'd all want to belong to that little 3%, so the question is: «How can you start to look at failure differently?»

Failure is not defeat: it is simply a lesson that teaches you that your current method isn't working. From there, you might need to revise your techniques or look again at the problem you're trying to resolve.

Let's take, for example, one of humanity's greatest accomplishments: flying.

Since time immemorial, man has wanted to sail through the air.

A thousand years ago, we were masters of the earth and sea – but we still hadn't conquered the sky. Without feathers or wings, it seemed like an impossible feat, and though the greatest thinkers of the era had insisted man would never fly – an eminently sound judgement – we couldn't shake the desire to do it.

Humans made hundreds of attempts to get off the ground – some comic, others tragic – but we never gave up, and something extraordinary began to happen: our failures were making each attempt better than the last. Finally, on December 17th 1903, brothers Orville and Wilbur Wright made the first manned flight in history. It lasted twelve seconds and covered one hundred and twenty feet.

After everything, we had achieved flight.

And what about the story of Thomas Edison and «his» lightbulb? Depending on who you ask, Thomas Edison was not the true inventor of the lightbulb, as others had already done it before him. But what others had invented were not commercially viable bulbs, and this was Edison's area of focus.

The solution didn't come quick or easy. Reports tell of thousands of failed attempts. But Edison never lost heart, and in 1880, he finally succeeded in producing the first commercially-viable lightbulb and left us with this famous quotation for posterity: «I have not failed. I've just found 10,000 ways that won't work.»

Temporary failure always precedes success. It doesn't prevent it. As such, you should look at failure as a springboard to success. Once you understand that failure is both temporary and impossible to avoid, you'll join that 3% of the population who can repeatedly succeed.

Fear of failure is a learned emotion, and like everything we learn, we can un-learn it. From now on, every time you face a setback or obstacle along the way and you notice the feeling of fear forming, apply these four steps:

1. Review

What caused the setback? Did you have wrong information? What factors had you not considered? A setback means something didn't go how you hoped it would, so you need to review your plan to work out where you went wrong or what you didn't account for.

2. Learn

Failure often means you need to patch up a gap in your knowledge, so you should try to acquire new skills or wisdom that can help you make a fresh and better attempt. It can also be very useful to look at what other people have done before you in order to succeed.

3. Adjust

«Insanity is doing the same thing over and over again and expecting different results.» –

Albert Einstein. You're not insane, though, so you can make adjustments to both your goals and your plans if you want your next attempt to be more successful. You have to find a new solution to the problem in front of you, and use this solution as a platform from which to try again.

4. Try again

You haven't failed until you stop trying. So you need to try again. A fresh attempt means you've changed your focus or that you have a better understanding of the problem and know what to do to avoid making the same mistakes. Even if you don't stumble upon the perfect solution right away, try again. Don't give up.

Learn to deal with criticism

One big problem we can face in life is called «learned helplessness». This term refers to the human (or animal) condition of having «learned» to behave passively, and the feeling of being incapable of doing anything or of responding to real opportunities to change an adverse situation around. Like many other problems we have, this condition is rooted in childhood. It goes from not acknowledging things a child does well, right to criticizing a child for everything they do wrong.

When a child's parents or guardians refuse to acknowledge or praise things the child does well, the child ends up feeling that they are not good enough. Since they aren't told that they just did something good, when the time comes to do it again, they choose not to – or, if they have no other option, they put less effort into it. This is because they think no how hard they try, they'll never be able to do it right.

This is learned helplessness, and many of us suffer from it without realizing. It stays with us from childhood right through to adulthood. It can be the root of poor self-esteem and lack of confidence. Learned helplessness is a feeling of ineptitude: the sense you'll never be good enough. In a way, this feeling stops you from setting goals for yourself – since you don't believe you deserve them – and it also saps any energy or motivation you might have to pursue those goals.

Fortunately, like any other learned condition, this behavior can be un-learned through self-appreciation. Every time you achieve a goal, no matter how small, your brain rewards you with feelings of pleasure, thanks to the release of what is known as «happiness hormones». You must savor these feelings. Keep a diary of your victories, big and small, to remind yourself of them when you need to. The idea is to embed this feeling of capability and adequacy into your subconscious, because once it's there, your actions will fall in line with it.

There will always be people who criticize you, whether you triumph or fail. Take note of constructive criticism and ignore toxic or destructive criticism. It's the best way to boost your self-esteem...and your sanity.

Chapter summary

Failure isn't the end. Giving up is. Success is usually the result of repeated failure. Setbacks are a necessary part of the equation; they tell you there's something you're doing wrong or not taking into account, and they enable you to make the necessary modifications to your plan. They are not confirmation of inadequacy; they simply filter out those who lack the motivation to keep going.

If you fall down seven times, get up eight!

- Every failure teaches you a lesson. Learn from your mistakes, and use them to get better.
- Failure is not definitive, nor is it permanent. With each failure, you learn a new way of not doing things, and you get closer and closer to your goals.

- Savor the pleasant sensation you get from achieving your aims, however small they may be, and your brain will absorb feelings of capability and self-sufficiency.

Conclusions

The road to success claims many victims along the way. Many are called, but few are chosen. Why is this?

Many people lack a clear image of what success entails. They have no goals; they live on autopilot, drifting aimlessly. They are moving, but not forward – they go in circles, with no real purpose.

Other people know exactly what their goals are, but don't have the map they need to get there. Instead of creating their own plans towards their aims, they continue to waste time on other people's plans. They embark on several plans at once, and they may end up getting to many places – but none of them are where they really want to be, and frustration ensues.

Some people have clearly-defined goals and the right map to reach them, but they lack the necessary motivation to do so. These people always throw in the towel halfway and abandon all their attempts. This is a particularly sad situation, as they may run out of steam when they are almost there. They might even encourage others and show them the way, but not be able to get there themselves. They know how to give the right advice; they just don't follow it.

Defeatists don't achieve their goals, either, because they give up in the face of failure and setbacks. They don't understand that failure exists to teach them a lesson, and instead of creating alternative solutions, they choose to give up and try their hand at something else. I don't think it's an exaggeration to say that people who give up fail in the most cowardly way possible.

If you want to succeed, you can't afford to fall into any of the above categories. You need a goal, a plan, motivation, and perseverance.

In this book, you have learned why you need a goal that gives you a destination. You should choose your goals for the right reasons if you want to stay focused and motivated. You also need a good plan, tailored to you, that can serve as a map to help you reach your goals little by little, setting smaller milestones that you keep passing until you reach your main objective. Motivation is non-negotiable; you must shape your way of thinking so that it becomes a vehicle to carry you to your destination. To do this, you need to surround yourself with the right people, learn to manage your time, and ensure your goals are in line with your principles and values. Finally, when obstacles present themselves, persevere and overcome them. You need to be flexible enough to avoid pitfalls without getting off track, while being firm enough to get through some of them when you have no other choice.

Always remember this:

Nothing can defeat a person with a destination, a map, motivation enough to succeed, and the willpower to get up after you fall.

The trip that changed my life. Thank you, Gili.

Your opinion matters

I hope you've enjoyed reading this book as much as I enjoyed writing it. This is my first book, and as a new author, I realize I set myself a big challenge: first, to write it, and then to publish it myself, without commercial backing. It has been a great adventure, and if you have a message to share with the world, I encourage you to give it a go. I really hope I have given you the knowledge you need to get your ideas across concisely and in an enjoyable way.

As an independent author, your opinion is really important to me, and **I would be hugely grateful if you could leave me a review** on Amazon to let me know what you thought of the book:

- What did you like the most?
- Did you find what you were looking for?
- Was there anything you thought should have been included?
- ...

In addition, if you are in any doubt about anything, don't hesitate to ask me in the review itself. I promise to respond as soon as I can.

Scan and leave a review

Take care!
Daniel

Other books by Daniel J. Martin

Get yours now

https://geni.us/psc-book

Printed in Great Britain
by Amazon